G000231705

WILLIE DOYLE SJ

'Much in the Presence of God'

Patrick Corkery SJ

First published in 2022 by Messenger Publications

Copyright © Patrick Corkery SJ, 2022

The right of Patrick Corkery SJ to be identified as the
author of the Work has been asserted by him in accordance with the
Copyright and Related Rights Act, 2000.

The material in this publication is protected by copyright law.
Except as may be permitted by law, no part of the material may be
reproduced (including by storage in a retrieval system) or transmitted in
any form or by any means, adapted, rented or lent without the written
permission of the copyright owners. Applications for permissions should
be addressed to the publisher.

ISBN: 9781788125512

Designed by Messenger Publications Design Department
Cover background image © KenDrysdale/Shutterstock
Typeset in Adobe Garamond Pro and Copperplate
Printed by GPS Colour Graphics

Messenger Publications,
37 Leeson Place, Dublin D02 E5V0, Ireland
www.messenger.ie

Dedication

This book is dedicated to the students of Gonzaga College SJ. I worked with them during my regency. Many of them took an interest in the project and often inquired about how the book was going. I am eternally grateful to them.

ACKNOWLEDGEMENTS

My thanks to Cecilia West, who invited me to write this booklet. I am fortunate with where I work and with my Jesuit community, so I am grateful to Damon McCaul, headmaster of Gonzaga College SJ, and Richard O'Dwyer SJ, superior of Gardiner Street Jesuit Community. I'm thankful to several Jesuits who looked at parts of this book while it was being written and gave me encouragement and feedback. My thanks to John James Braithwaite SJ, Patrick Carberry SJ, Niall Leahy SJ, Dermot Mansfield SJ, Bernard McGuckian SJ, Thomas Morrissey SJ, James Murphy SJ and Michael Sheil SJ. My special thanks to the Fr Willie Doyle Association, members of which helped me with numerous things throughout the writing of this booklet. I am grateful to a number of my friends who looked at parts of the text and offered helpful advice, thanks to Claire Reid, Eilís Regan and Tomás Miller. Finally, thanks to my family and friends for their encouragement in general.

CONTENTS

Introduction 7

Willie Doyle's Early Life 10

Willie Doyle Joins the Jesuits 14

Willie Doyle's Journey to the Priesthood 21

Willie Doyle's Discernment and Spirituality 30

Willie Doyle and the First World War 41

What Can Willie Doyle Teach People Today? 51

INTRODUCTION

FR WILLIE DOYLE has haunted me for several years. Before I entered the Jesuits, his name popped up on occasion. When I was a candidate for the Jesuits, I came across a story about a Benedictine convent in the United Kingdom that had long hoped for an Irish vocation. The nuns began a novena to Fr Willie Doyle, and the day the novena concluded, an Irish visitor arrived at the convent. Several years later, she and two subsequent young women became members of that community. While some people might find novenas twee or think them out of kilter with contemporary spirituality, it is clear that Fr Willie Doyle has an attraction for people and devotion to him remains strong.

Hearing about the success of this novena, I began to invoke Fr Doyle in my prayers while making my application to the Jesuits. I had flicked through Alfred O'Rahilly's monumental work on Fr Doyle during my discernment process; while it did not impact my choice to enter, I was struck by Fr Doyle's zeal and commitment to religious life. At times his penances were off-putting, but one could not help but admire how dedicated he was to the people he served, and how Fr Doyle desired to make God known to those with whom he interacted. This spirit seemed very much in tune with the other heroic Jesuit saints I read about during this period of discernment.

Before embarking on the formation period known as regency, I was recommended to look at Alfred O'Rahilly's book once more. I found myself drawn to Fr Doyle's time in formation and, in particular, the time he spent in Clongowes Wood College in County Kildare. Here O'Rahilly depicted a time of great activity in Fr Doyle's life, when he threw himself entirely into his work and made himself available to the students he served. Reading about this lit a fire inside of me as I prepared for my regency; I wanted to hand myself over to this process and try to give myself completely to those I would serve. While I can't claim to be as prodigious as Fr Doyle, I often thought of how he was there for his students, and I hope that I have imitated something of his attitude of service during my regency.

At the beginning of regency, my provincial asked me to assist a lay group formed to promote Fr Doyle's canonisation cause. I don't know if the provincial knew about my interest in Fr Doyle, but it certainly helped strengthen my devotion to him and helped me see that Ireland potentially has a great saint relevant for our time. In being asked by Messenger Publications to write this booklet, I hoped to capture something of Fr Doyle's significance for a modern audience. Too often, historical figures are left trapped in their time, their contemporary relevance obscured by our attitude toward the time period they lived in. Fr Doyle has suffered from this problem in certain quarters. His harsh personal penances seem to paint him as an aloof and severe figure. I hope to change this narrative, which I think does little justice to a remarkable man.

Let me quote from one of Fr Doyle's personal prayers that captures the essence of the Christian life.

'Come, O Holy Ghost into my heart and make me
holy so that I may be generous with God
and become a saint.'

WILLIE DOYLE'S EARLY LIFE

THERE IS something within the human condition that is drawn towards tragic events. People can find comfort in the heroism of those who overcome a difficult start and go on to live fulfilling lives. This story doesn't begin with tragedy; it starts in a stable home in the seaside village of Dalkey in County Dublin. Willie Doyle was born on 3 March 1873. He was the youngest of seven children of Hugh and Christine Doyle. His older brother, Charles (Charlie), became his inseparable childhood companion. The two boys spent much of their time together playing soldiers and cricket. They enjoyed harmless pranks, though these pranks may not have been enjoyed by those on the receiving end of them.

Willie Doyle's parents were equally loving and showered a good deal of attention on their children. They instilled in their children the values common in their day, ensuring that their children were well catechised in the Catholic faith, which was essential to all the family. This early introduction to the faith profoundly affected the young Willie and sparked a strong social conscience within him. From a young age, he took a strong interest in the local poor; he would visit their homes and even parted with his meagre pocket money to ensure that they were able to enjoy some small luxuries. Stories of young Willie's generosity entered in family lore and were recounted later in his brother Charlie's biography of Willie, *Merry In God*.

In one famous story, the young Willie was given money by an uncle and instructed to treat himself. On the way to a pastry shop, he came across a beggar, and a moral dilemma emerged. Would he treat himself, or would he hand over the money? The child wrestled with the desire to have sweets – he had a sweet tooth – and the impulse to give the money to someone in greater need than himself. Reluctantly he parted with the money, and he returned home empty-handed and downcast. When his uncle learned about the child's sacrifice, he gifted him more money. In the end, Willie got his cake and learned something about making sacrifices to help others. This lesson was to form the core of his life and ministry.

This early introduction to the faith profoundly affected the young Willie and sparked a strong social conscience within him.

Thanks to his father's job, the Doyle family was comfortable. Hugh Doyle served as chief clerk of the high court of bankruptcy. This allowed the Doyle's certain luxuries, which would set them apart from many in Irish society at the time. This luxury did not mean that the Doyles were alienated from the realities faced by many of their neighbours. Even domestically, Willie sought to make life easier for the family's servants. He would often rise early in the morning before the domestic staff and complete some of the tasks allotted to them. This was never done in a showy way but always quietly and never seeking any reward. His care and concern for others and his desire to be of service were evident early in life.

In 1884 Willie was sent to boarding school in England. He entered Ratcliffe College, run by the Institute of Charity but colloquially known as the Rosminians. From what is known, Willie seemed to enjoy his time in boarding school. He was not a gifted academic but worked to the best of his abilities. He appears to have excelled in the social dimension of school life; he threw himself vigorously into the sporting life of the college and played cricket and football. His older brother, Charlie, who was ahead of him at Ratcliffe, noted that Willie's sporting prowess and good humour helped to make him one of the more popular students in the college. Young Willie appears to have had an easy-going nature that attracted others to him, and they enjoyed being in his company. This ease in the company of others seems to have been a trait from early on.

TIME TO REFLECT

Looking at Willie's early life might help you to reflect on where you are at right now in your life. Perhaps this is a good time to pause, reflect and ask some questions.

1. Willie learned the tenets of the faith in his family home. What from your early faith do you still treasure? Are there prayers or images from your childhood that still enrich and nourish your spiritual life?
2. Willie had a strong social conscience. Charity is a crucial gospel value. How do you live out this gospel value in your own life?
3. Reflecting on your early life, who are the people you are grateful for? Who are the people who helped make you the person you are today?

WILLIE DOYLE JOINS THE JESUITS

WILLIE FINISHED at Ratcliffe in 1890, and no one was surprised when he announced he wanted to be a priest; the question that followed was where would he serve as a priest? Of the seven Doyle children, four opted for religious life, including Willie. His oldest brother, Fred, had initially been a Jesuit but left to join the Archdiocese of Dublin. Charlie, who was his closest sibling, had entered the Jesuit novitiate and persisted in that vocation, becoming a priest and at one point was assistant to the Jesuit provincial in Ireland. He would also play a role in helping to develop the spirituality of Frank Duff, founder of the Legion of Mary. Willie's sister, May, entered the Sisters of Mercy, taking the religious name Benedict. Having multiple children was not uncommon in Irish families at this time, and it was considered a mark of great pride to have children enter religious life. The prayerful atmosphere of the Doyle home no doubt contributed to multiple vocations.

Fred's vocation as a diocesan priest had a considerable impact on Willie. Fred had been studying for the priesthood in Rome, where he contracted a fever and died in March 1887. Fred was only a few days away from being ordained a priest, and the suddenness of his death was a hard blow for the whole family. Willie felt the sense of loss and felt called to the diocesan priesthood, hoping in some way to replace Fred's vocation. This way of thinking may seem strange, but it is very much part of Willie's dutiful nature. He seemed set on becoming a diocesan priest and was dismissive of alternatives suggested to him. Charlie had other ideas and invited Willie to come and visit him at the Jesuit novitiate at St Stanislaus College (Tullabeg) in County Offaly. Willie was not impressed by what he saw of the Jesuit novitiate and told his brother, 'I would never come to this hole of a place'.[1] Even this staunch proclamation did not deter Charlie, and on departing, he gifted his brother a book on the religious life.

The book Willie received from Charlie was *The Religious State: together with a Short Treatise on the Vocation to the Priesthood* by St Alphonsus Liguori. In this book, St Alphonsus outlines the importance of a vocation to the religious life and argues that it is the perfect confirmation to God's will. The book seems to have profoundly affected Willie, and he began to reconsider his options. As he discerned between the diocese and Jesuits, he became more drawn to the latter. On Christmas Day 1890, Willie made up his mind. He would write about this transformation saying, 'I was in the drawing-room at the piano when father came in and asked me if I had yet made up my mind as to my future career. I answered, "Yes" – that I intended

1   Charlie Doyle, *Merry in God: A Life of Father William Doyle SJ* (London: Longmans, Green and Co., 1939), 44.

to become a Jesuit. I remember how I played my joy and happiness into the piano, after thus giving myself openly to Jesus.'[2]

The Jesuits had been at Tullabeg since 1818 and St Stanislaus College had served in a variety of different capacities. It had been a boarding school, house of formation for Jesuits and eventually served as a retreat house before it closed in 1991. Despite his initial hesitation about Tullabeg, Willie wrote about his arrival in glowing terms, 'I remember well my arrival at Tullabeg and the way I astonished the Father Socius[3] (as he told me afterwards) by running up to the hall door three steps at a time. He was not accustomed, he said, to see novices coming in such a merry mood, evidently enjoying the whole thing; and though I did not know it then, it was the best signs of a real vocation.'[4]

For some, the Jesuit formation process may need some explanation. There are multiple stages to Jesuit formation: novitiate, juniorate, philosophy, regency, theology, and if one opts to be a priest, there is ordination. The Jesuits also have lay-brothers who do not get ordained. However, brothers have the same vows[5] as priests and work to contribute to the mission of the Society of Jesus. After some time at work in their ministries, brothers and priests return to a final period of formation called tertianship. This is like a second novitiate, and afterwards, they take final vows.

2 Doyle, *Merry in God*, 45.
3 The assistant to the novice master.
4 Doyle, *Merry in God*, 45.
5 A Jesuit takes three vows: poverty, chastity and obedience.

16

This formation process has remained almost the same since the Jesuits were founded in 1540. The formation of a Jesuit can take up to fifteen years.

Those who know about the Jesuits will probably be familiar with the heroic lives of Jesuits who, often in dire circumstances, proclaimed the love of God. This active life is in sharp contrast to what awaits a prospective Jesuit novice. Life comes to a standstill as the novices adjust to a slower pace of being. This change of pace allows the novice time to reflect upon vocation and learn to exist in the mundane aspects of religious life. In Willie Doyle's time, novices were given 'experiments' in the kitchen, helping with the washing up and cooking, and in the infirmary, tending to the ill. These experiments were designed to help the novice grow closer to life's ordinary tasks. These experiments still exist in modern times but have become more worldly, with some novices being sent to minister in the Global South.

There are multiple stages to Jesuit formation: novitiate, juniorate, philosophy, regency, theology, and if one opts to be a priest, there is ordination.

Despite arriving happily in Tullabeg and gaining great fruit from the Spiritual Exercises, Willie encountered a moment of crisis that threatened his vocation. A fire broke out in St Stanislaus College, and while he escaped from the fire, Willie seems to have been traumatised by the event. The trauma of the event resulted in his being sent home from the novitiate. Such an event would typically have spelt the end of a vocation. Still, Willie's superiors were assured he was called to be a Jesuit and invited him back to Tullabeg following a period of recuperation. This mental breakdown must have been immense for Willie, given his later heroism during the war. Coming so close to death almost ended his time as a Jesuit and damaged his mental state. In recovering, Willie found a new sense of peace within himself, and his superiors indeed recognised something in him, as they chose not to dismiss him.

I don't know the emotions that Willie felt, or what he went through at this time. Breakdowns are commonplace in the world today. Everyone knows someone who has gone through some form of mental anguish that has caused them to take time for themselves. Though it is possible to empathise with the pain and the hurt someone is going through, it may not be possible to understand it. Suffering is something society seems to shut out. The focus is on the positives and times when crises emerge are neglected. Willie shared in this suffering and came out the other side. Not only did he arise from the breakdown, but he was also able to sit with others in times of trouble and provide them with comfort. Willie did not live in his wounds; he lived with them and used them to help others.

On 15 August 1893, Willie Doyle took his vows and became a Jesuit. Earlier in that year he had made his own personal vow to Mary, writing, 'My Martyrdom for Mary's Sake. Darling Mother Mary, in preparation for the glorious martyrdom which I feel assured thou art going to obtain for me, I, thy most unworthy child, oh this the first day of thy month, solemnly commence my life of slow martyrdom by earnest hard work and constant self-denial. With my blood I promise thee to keep this resolution, do thou, sweet Mother, assist me and obtain for me the one favour I wish and long for: To die a Jesuit Martyr. May God's will, not mine, be done! May 1st, 1893. Amen.'[6]

The modern reader may be shocked by Willie's vow. The squeamish reader may recoil at his commitment to signing his vow in blood. It is important, however, to understand the time in which Willie lived. Novices would have devoured the lives of the Jesuit saints and martyrs during this period. Stories of saints like Andrew Bobola[7] or the North American martyrs[8] would have sparked the imagination of the novices. They would have sought to emulate these men and to follow them to the ends of the earth in proclaiming the Gospel. These men led holy lives under great strain. Yes, their lives were also exceptional – many Jesuits lived and worked quietly in schools or parish missions – but they nonetheless fuelled the imaginations of novices dreaming of adventure.

6   Alfred O'Rahilly, *Father William Doyle SJ* (London: Longmans, Green and Co., 1922), 10.
7   Polish Jesuit martyred by Cossacks in Eastern Europe.
8   French missionaries martyred by Native Americans in North America.

TIME TO REFLECT

Willie struggled with his vocation. This is a good place to stop and reflect on the topic of vocation and the struggles people can experience in life.

1. Ignatius was inspired to pursue a new life by reading the *Lives of the Saints*. Similarly, a book made a meaningful impact on the journey of the young Willie Doyle. Have any books made a similar impact on your faith journey?
2. God calls all people to some form of service in this life. Each person has their own way of serving God and a vocation that is unique to them. What vocation has God called you to? How have you lived out this vocation?
3. Willie's breakdown is familiar. Many people struggle under the burden of mental illness. Have you ever found yourself in such a struggle? If so, how did you cope at the time? What, if anything, about struggle and mental health can you learn from the life of Willie Doyle?

WILLIE DOYLE'S JOURNEY TO THE PRIESTHOOD

UNDER NORMAL circumstances, Willie would have progressed to juniorate, where he would have engaged in some form of academic training, or he might have been sent to philosophy as part of his priestly training. His fragile health made his superiors take an unusual step and send him to work in one of the Jesuit schools; in this instance, he was sent to Clongowes Wood College in County Kildare. Clongowes is the motherhouse of the Irish Jesuits, having been established in 1814. It continues to serve as an all-boys boarding school. Willie would spend a considerable period of his life in Clongowes, initially from 1894–1898 and again from 1901–1903. Clongowes would also become home to Blessed John Sullivan, whose association with the college is still remembered. Willie's impact on the life of the college is significant, though it is less often acknowledged.

His time at Clongowes positively affected the students, and his legacy continues in the form of the Clongowes Past Pupils Union, the Clongowes annual musical and the *Old Clongowegian* magazine. These staples of college life all owe their inception to Willie, who threw himself vigorously into promoting new things and immersing himself in the lives of his students. Willie also took an active role in the college's sporting life. He acted as a prefect, and one of his students remembers his time in that role, 'I first met Fr Doyle when I was a small boy at Clongowes. He was then Third Line Prefect[9], and had under his care some seventy or eighty boys ranging from ten to fifteen years of age. This particular set were rowdy and quarrelsome, and during my first year in the Line there were two periods, at least, of acute disturbance. Not that the trouble circled round Fr Doyle or was directed against him, nor was it caused by any act on his part, but arose out of feuds among the boys themselves. The manner in which Fr Doyle dealt with this difficult situation impressed me even at the time, and I have been more deeply impressed again and again in retrospection. Hot tempered by nature, I believe, he never allowed himself to be carried into arbitrary action by the intemperate or unreasonable conduct of those in his charge. He was firm, but never unjust; indeed, if he erred at all, it was on the side of leniency. But apart from his self-control, the quality that struck me most was his optimism, his breezy cheerfulness in the midst of difficulties. He never lost his good spirits;

9   For those not familiar with this system, I was given an insight to its meaning by the current rector of Clongowes, Fr Michael Sheil: 'Clongowes is run along 3 horizontal "Lines", where Third Line is for first & second years (12–14), Lower Line is the middle of the school (14–16) and Higher Line is the senior part (16–18). This system came to Clongowes from Stonyhurst College in England. Remember that Peter Kenney was at school in Stonyhurst. It was probably he who introduced these terms, which still exist today (although all the prefects are lay). In the past the TLP [Third Line Prefect] used to be a Jesuit scholastic doing his regency [working in a college or on the missions] while in formation. The prefect is the housemaster and is in loco parentis. He is responsible for the general well-being of the students in his care – just as a parent would be – his remit extends to everything outside the strictly academic side of boarding school life.'

he never seemed to be he never appeared to consider for a moment how trouble in his department affected himself; he was intent always on setting others on the right track.'[10]

When Willie was at Clongowes, corporal punishment was part of the everyday life of the school. Willie's 'leniency' sheds light on his character. His desire to serve others undoubtedly moved him toward leniency. He always erred on the side of compassion. However hard he was on himself, he never allowed this to affect those under his care. His former student emphasised this, despite his 'hot tempered' nature, Willie was never unjust. Not all priests and religious were lenient in their care of others. Willie was authentically trying to imitate Jesus. He treated those he met with a Christian tenderness.

Another of his students echoed these sentiments, 'Fr Doyle's example worked good. His cheerfulness, his energy, his enthusiasm were infectious and inspiring. His whole conduct was marked by gentleness and a kindly thoughtfulness that gained him loyalty and affection. In the playing fields he was a tower of strength. I can still recall the admiration with which I watched him play full back, or stump a batsman who had his toe barely off the ground. But above all he gave the impression to us boys of one who lived much in the presence of God. I know one boy, at least, who entered the Society of Jesus, partly, at any rate, because Fr Doyle was such a splendid man and splendid Jesuit.'[11]

While his time in Clongowes looks a lot like a modern

10   O'Rahilly, *Father William*, 13.
11   O'Rahilly, *Father William*, 14.

Jesuit regency, it was nonetheless a test for Willie. His superiors were testing his health to see if he could survive the strain of working in a busy environment. Willie passed this test and was sent to study philosophy in 1898. Initially, he was sent to Belgium, but concerns for his health saw him move to England after a year. He continued his philosophy at Stonyhurst College in Lancashire. His time in England coincided with the Boer War, when Britain fought Dutch settlers in South Africa for control. The Boer War foregrounded Willie's politics. Irish sympathies tended to lie with the Boers, and Willie was no exception. A Dutch Jesuit recounted to Charlie Doyle, 'I knew Fr Willie from 1890–1901 at Stonyhurst. What I best remember about him is that he was very kind, very cheerful, that he was a keen footballer, and that after Sir Redvers Buller's Tugela adventure he came shouting down our corridor, "Hurrah! The British have lost six guns!" Yet such was his popularity, and he had such a way with him, that the most patriotic Englishmen took no offence.'[12]

Willie was able to keep the affection of those who knew him well even when they differed politically. After his philosophy studies, he returned to Clongowes and spent time in Belvedere College in Dublin (1901–1904). In both places, he was well regarded as is recorded by a contemporary, 'A fellow religious who lived with him during his last years in the colleges, and who was in America at the time of his death, wrote "I can safely say he was a perfect

12 Doyle, *Merry in God*, 67.

Jesuit and often reminded me of St John Berchmans.[13] His was a combination of real solid piety with a truly human character. Bright and joyous himself, he always made others happy and was evidently happy to be able to do so. To those who knew his self-sacrificing devotedness there could be no doubt as to the identity of the heroic Irish Padre the first despatches recording his death spoke of. So certain was I, that I told my friends here that the hero was Fr Willie.'[14]

Willie was sent to theology in September 1904. He studied in Milltown Park, the Jesuit theologate in Dublin. O'Rahilly notes that Willie found studies difficult and was sometimes bored by what he had to read. He also says that ill health during his time in philosophy had a negative effect on Willie's theology studies. It is important to note that Willie often clashed with his superiors. He could sometimes be stubborn, and his sense of humour was not always appreciated. For one thing, he would mimic other Jesuits. A famous story of him dressing a mannequin in a Jesuit gown and throwing it out a window entered Jesuit folklore. The prank was intended to make colleagues walking outside think that he'd fallen

---

13 Berchmans was a Belgian Jesuit who died during his studies and is now a saint.
14 O'Rahilly, *Father William*, 21.

out a window after he waved to them. Such stunts left a bitter taste in the mouths of some of his contemporaries.

Carol Hope in her book *Worshipper and Worshipped* talks about 'his impetuous character, often leading to a rebuke or even punishment for lack of respect. Several times at Milltown Park Willie got into trouble when he was unable to resist poking fun at those in authority. One such occasion was when one of the older Fathers had been particularly vexatious and it was Willie's turn to read the daily menology at supper (a menology is a listing of saints, often with brief biographies, arranged in calendar order.) Instead of reading the entry for a deceased member of the Society, Willie's obituary was a humorous caricature of the offending Father who was actually present in the refectory.'[15]

Hope also notes some other transgressions, 'On another occasion he was ordered to his room by his Superior, a school boy's punishment for a man just into his third decade! Willie obeyed: but instead of shutting his door, he piled up chair, table, priedieu, etc., at the entrance and during the evening interviewed and entertained friends and sympathisers from behind the barrier.'[16]

When he and his peers believed that there had been an injustice or that a new regulation was unfair, Willie challenged his superiors. For instance, he reacted angrily when a somewhat officious lay brother had locked a gate leading into a field that the theology students routinely had access to. Willie smashed the lock to restore the right of way

15 Carol Hope, *Worshipper and Worshipped* (London: Reveille Press, 2013), 83.
16 Hope, *Worshipper and Worshipped*, 84.

and incurred the wrath of his superiors. Charlie comments, 'For this he justly got a reprimand and a penance, because a religious subject may not take the law into his own hands even to right a wrong.'[17] A rare criticism from Charlie!

Willie's sense of humour was a point of contention later in life. Many of his Irish contemporaries only remember his pranks, which did not endear him to them. His poor connection with some of his Jesuit colleagues is in sharp contrast to the affection that members of the public held him in. His esteem among Jesuits grew as he matured, but those who failed to get to know him were slow to abandon their earlier prejudices. Despite some difficult moments with his superiors, Willie was approved for ordination and was ordained in July 1907. He was ordained the same year as Blessed John Sullivan. However, there is no record of what either man thought of the other.

Willie wrote to his sister before his ordination. From his letter you can get a sense of his state of mind leading up to this big event.

> I can scarcely believe I have all the long years of study, which I used to dread so much, really over. You know I was never intended by Almighty God to keep my nose buried in books all days. Climbing up chimneys, or walking on my head across the roof of a house, is more in my line! When I came here three years ago, my health was anything but good, and kind friends said I would not spend six

17 Hope, *Worshipper and Worshipped*, 84.

weeks at theology. But after the first Christmas things began to improve and, thank God, have gone on improving steadily ever since, so that now, in spite of the hard work – and it has been hard and trying – I am in far better health and able to do more than when I came here. I look upon this as a great grace from God, and I only hope I shall not prove ungrateful to Him for all He has done …

As you may imagine, all my thoughts at present are centred on the Great Day, July 28th. The various events of the year have helped to keep it before my mind, learning to say Mass, the Divine Office etc.; but now that such a short time remains, I find it hard to realise that I shall be a priest so very soon. Were it not for all the good prayers, sister mine, which are being offered up daily for me, I should almost feel in despair, because these long years of waiting (nearly seventeen now) have only brought home to me how unworthy I am of such an honour and dignity.[18]

Now Willie Doyle was a priest, and his mission would take on a new dimension, one which would help mould him into becoming the heroic chaplain of the First World War.

18   Doyle, *Merry in God*, 73.

TIME TO REFLECT

There are times in life when people go through great change. Let's stop and think about this formative period in Willie's life.

1. For many of his students, Willie seems to have been that 'one good adult', can you think of adults in your childhood who played this role in your development?
2. Willie Doyle struggled throughout his life. Academically he was not brilliant, and his health plagued him. These setbacks proved to be more formative than destructive. Can you think of times when you overcame obstacles that might have otherwise held you back?
3. Not everyone enjoyed Willie's sense of humour. Perhaps there are things about you that others do not appreciate. Can you accept that people are different to you? Can you learn not to judge people for being different to you?

WILLIE DOYLE'S DISCERNMENT
AND SPIRITUALITY

AFTER BEING ordained, Willie was sent to Belgium, where he would undergo yet more Jesuit formation. The tertianship was designed to reacquaint the newly ordained priest (or brother who had spent some time in formation) with certain principles of Jesuit life. Once again, they would undergo the Spiritual Exercises and engage in missionary work. It was a second novitiate in a certain sense and was meant to act as a grounding and final incorporation into the Jesuit way of proceeding. Willie's tertianship seems to have been a blessed time for him; in particular he left extensive notes on his experience of the Spiritual Exercises, where Ignatian discernment helped him to chart his future as a priest.

Ignatian discernment is not a matter of choosing between good and bad. It isn't a matter of say choosing between robbing a bank or giving money to charity – there is only one choice there, and it isn't robbing a bank. Ignatian discernment is often about choosing between two goods. Two things can both bring a person closer to faith. In Willie's case, he wanted to be a missionary in Africa, but he also knew he could do good staying in Ireland. He worked this desire out in his diary in the way recommended by Ignatius. Willie's discernment looked like this.

REASONS AGAINST

1. I am not certain of the will of God.
2. I should like to remain for some years in Ireland and work for souls.
3. Should I not do more good by remaining in Ireland instead of burying myself among a few Africans whose language I do not know ?
4. I may have a long useful life at home; on the mission probably a very short one.

REASONS FOR

1. The almost certain conviction that I have a real vocation for the foreign mission.
2. This thought has been in my mind for over twenty years and the thought of it has given me great pleasure and consolation.
3. My desire, even as a boy, to be a martyr.
4. The letter I wrote as a novice.
5. The feeling that, if I do not offer myself, I certainly shall not please God.
6. The attraction I feel for a life of real privation and suffering.
7. This is much stronger since the retreat, in order to be more like Jesus.

8. In the spirit of the Third Degree I should make this sacrifice.
9. The hardship of the life, a great help to holiness.
10. The attraction the life of St Peter Claver[19] has always had for me, my desire to imitate him.
11. The souls I shall be able to save, and who otherwise would never see heaven.
12. As an English-speaking priest I may be of help to the missionaries.
13. I feel quite content that I was doing God's will when I resolved two years ago to offer myself for the foreign mission.[20]

Willie's train of thought was well worked out. He saw himself being of more service to God on the missions than if he remained in Ireland. Since the time of St Francis Xavier[21], the Church's desire to evangelise outside of Europe had captured the minds of many Jesuits. Willie had a strong devotion to Xavier and wanted to imitate him. While they appear outmoded in the twenty-first century, such desires were at the heart of many Jesuit vocations throughout much of the twentieth century and before. Willie believed he might be of service and recognised that he had weaknesses that could hinder the mission. In the end, he was convinced this was God's will for him. He wrote about it, saying, 'To-

19 A Spanish Jesuit missionary who worked to help slaves in the Spanish colonial empire.
20 O'Rahilly, *Father William*, 53–54.
21 A Spanish Jesuit missionary in Asia. He spent considerable time working in India, he also worked in Japan. He died hoping to travel to China.

day the First Friday of November, the Feast of All Saints, I made my election about offering myself for the Congo Mission. During the retreat I have been praying and thinking over this, asking for light to know God's holy will which alone I seek.'[22]

Jesuit discernment may involve a person coming to their own conclusions about what God may want. They might be convinced that God has a particular path in mind for them. In the end, however, they may come to see God has a different plan in store for them. This can be seen in the life of Ignatius, who wanted to be a missionary in the Holy Land, a desire that was not fulfilled. You can also see it in the life of Willie Doyle as well. His desire to go to the Congo never materialised. Even though he desired to be a missionary, Willie understood that God's will was paramount. This is not an uncommon feature of discernment. In such cases the discerning person must trust that whatever happens is the will of God, though they may not see it in that moment, and hand themselves over entirely in God's providence. Sometimes you and I may be more inclined to pray that 'my will be done' rather than 'thy will be done'.

After tertianship, Willie spent some additional time at Belvedere College. In 1910 he was moved into parish retreats and would remain in this ministry until 1915. This work involved going to various parishes in Ireland and Britain. There he would preach, meet members of the public in their homes, celebrate Mass and most importantly,

22   O'Rahilly, *Father William*, 54.

hear confessions. Willie greatly loved the ministry of reconciliation and knew that many people could encounter Christ's healing love through confession. His gentle manner and sense of humour would likely have attracted many people to seek him out in the confessional during these missions. His work in the confessional undoubtedly helped many people understand that God loved and cherished them.

Between 1908 and 1915 Willie Doyle gave over 150 parish missions. Given the time and preparation involved in this work, this was a considerable achievement. His missionary zeal was not confined to being active; he understood that any missionary endeavour also required a commitment to prayer. In his letters to his family, he cites moments where he was tired or downcast about the prospects of his parish missions. In such moments he always recognised that such inclinations were not the product of the Holy Spirit. Drawing on the Spiritual Exercises, Willie knew that in coming up against spiritual discouragement, one should turn to God for guidance. Self-reliance was not sufficient when facing such doubts. In the Exercises, Ignatius recommended the person turn to God for assistance. Willie regularly did this through long periods of personal prayer.

Willie also contributed to other aspects of the Jesuit mission in Ireland during this time. From his time in Belgium, he saw the importance of retreats for lay people, in particular, for those from a lower socio-economic background. Willie was attached to this idea and petitioned the Irish provincial to embark on such work in Ireland. The province eventually purchased Rathfarnham Castle for this purpose, but Willie Doyle would never see his ambition come to fruition. At Rathfarnham Castle, countless lay people would come to know the transformative power of Ignatius's Spiritual Exercises. Vocations also occupied Willie's attention, and he wrote two pamphlets on the topic. He writes about this decision in a letter to a family member.

You will be glad to know (90,000 copies) of my little book *Vocations* is rapidly being exhausted. After my ordination, when I began to be consulted on this important subject, I was struck by the fact that there was nothing one could put into the hands of boys and girls to help them to a decision, except ponderous volumes, which they would scarcely read. Even the little treatise by St Liguori which Fr Charles gave me during my first visit to Tullabeg, and which changed the whole current of my thoughts, was out of print. I realized the want for some time; but one evening as I walked back to the train after dining with you, the thought of the absolute necessity for such a book seized me so strongly, (I could almost point out the exact spot on the road), that there and then I made up my mind to persuade someone to write it, for I never dreamt of even attempting the task myself. I soon found out that the shortest way to get a thing done is to do it yourself, or rather God in His goodness had determined to make use of me, because I was lacking in the necessary qualifications, to get His work done, for I am firmly convinced that both in *Vocations* and *Shall I be a Priest?* the venerable manager of the Messenger Office began shaking his head over the prospect of its selling, for as he said with truth, it is a subject which appeals to a limited few. He decided to print 5,000, and hinted I might buy them all.[23]

Despite the scepticism of the Messenger Office, Willie's pamphlets became very popular. Sales exceeded all expectations during his lifetime, and this popularity continued long after his death. In writing this booklet I spoke to the President of the Fr Willie Doyle Association. The Association runs a blog on Willie Doyle, which is an important resource. As manager of the blog the President receives numerous testimonies about Willie Doyle from all over the world. In one case he heard from a priest who had been a veteran of the Second World War. During the war he had been given one of Willie's pamphlets by an army chaplain. It eventually inspired him to enter the priesthood. Later in life he thanked the chaplain for the pamphlet and was told, 'You're the twelfth man who has told me they became a priest because of that pamphlet.'

23 O'Rahilly, *Father William*, 81.

Willie Doyle's Spirituality

Writing about Willie Doyle over a hundred years after his death can pose problems. Willie was a product of his time and lived in a time that contemporary readers may not readily understand. What may seem strange to the contemporary reader was perfectly normal to Willie and those around him. One source of controversy attached to Willie was his penances. These are a continuing source of fuel for would-be critics. His penances were severe, but they were not different from the kind of penances adopted by other holy people throughout history, such as John Vianney[24] or Matt Talbot[25]. Willie's penances are often challenging because they show a level of fortitude that others may not readily share in.

He would deprive himself of food and sleep very often. He would engage in corporal punishments regularly. He constantly sought to reject comfort and experience painful circumstances in the desire to gain greater holiness. Such penances do not appeal to me, perhaps because I know I don't have the stamina for them, and I do not believe God is calling me to such a severe way of living. I can't dispute that God may call others to this way of life and has done since the early Church. When Willie undertook these penances, he never operated alone. Willie always consulted his provincial and spiritual director to ensure he had their blessing. This strict personal regime was never one he forced

24 French priest famous for his work in the confessional.
25 Dublin lay man who gave up alcohol and led a hidden life of charity and service to others.

on other people. His advice to others was always gentle, and he drew upon the wisdom of people like Peter Faber[26] and Thérèse of Lisieux[27]. In doing so, he encouraged people to find God in the little things in life.

His personality was attractive those who came in contact with him. Despite his severity toward himself, he could still gain the affection and adoration of others. This says something about how he behaved in his day-to-day life. His penances are recorded in his spiritual journals. He had expected these to be destroyed when he died. Knowledge of them is only possible because these texts remain. Had they not existed, no one would know of Willie's inner life. Instead, study of Willie would depend on the testimonies of those who actually knew him. And these people continually praised his character and portrayed him warmly.

Is there a way for a modern reader to understand the nature of Willie's penances? I tend to think of them as a kind of preparation for the depravation of the trenches. In the horrific conditions of the First World War, scarcely imaginable to you and me, Willie was able to maintain good spirits and provide spiritual and material comfort to the suffering.

An important part of Willie's interior life was his devotion to Mary and the saints. This mirrored many Jesuits of the time and Ignatius in particular. Above all he had a great reverence for Jesus and understood him most

---

26 Early companion of St Ignatius, was made a saint by Pope Francis.
27 French Carmelite nun, born the same year as Willie Doyle. He was greatly taken by her life and spiritual counsel.

profoundly within the context of the Sacred Heart. The Sacred Heart was popularised following a series of visions by a French Visitation Sister, St Margaret Mary Alacoque. She was presented in the seventeenth century with a series of revelations regarding the Sacred Heart of Jesus, who, among other things, told her, 'My Divine Heart is so inflamed with love'. At first, St Margaret Mary believed she was suffering from insanity and rejected the visions. She changed her mind only after the vision told her that someone would come to help her promote what she had seen. That person was a Jesuit priest, Fr Claude de la Colombière, whom the beatific vision described as 'my faithful servant and perfect friend'. Prompted by Fr de la Colombière's example, a connection developed between Jesuits and the promotion of the Sacred Heart.

The devotion's timing was providential. It did much to curtail the rigid excesses of Jansenism in France, which was prominent at the time. Jansenists sought to portray the Jesuits as being too lax on sin and opposed the Jesuits encouraging people to frequent communion. In this climate, the Sacred Heart acted as a reminder of Jesus' love and mercy against the strictures of Jansenism. Throughout his life Willie was a faithful promoter of this devotion through two Jesuit ministries, the Apostleship of Prayer (today called the Pope's Worldwide Prayer Network) and the Pioneer Total Abstinence Association of the Sacred Heart.

TIME TO REFLECT

Willie threw himself into his work after he was ordained. It's time to pause and reflect on his experience of discernment and the practise of his spirituality.

1. Discernment is an essential part of the spirituality of Ignatius. How have you practised discernment in your life? Have you ever made an important decision using the 'for' and 'against' model Ignatius recommends?

2. Jesus became known to Willie Doyle through the Sacred Heart devotion. Do personal devotions play a role in your spirituality? If so, how?

3. Reading about Willie Doyle's penances may be challenging. In seasons like Advent or Lent, you are encouraged to make sacrifices to help you grow in your relationship with God. These sacrifices aren't like Willie's, but they can bring insight. How has giving something up or taking something on in a religious context affected your relationship with God?

WILLIE DOYLE AND
THE FIRST WORLD WAR

IN JULY 1914, Archduke Franz Ferdinand and his wife were assassinated in Sarajevo. The event was to have a cataclysmic effect on European politics. Within months the major European powers were at war, including the United Kingdom, which meant Ireland found itself at war too. Many politicians predicted a short war, but setbacks to the German Army in the late Summer meant that the war, which was expected to be over by Christmas, dragged into 1915. Initially marked by great movement, the war descended into a stalemate. Both armies sat in trenches stretching from the Channel to the Swiss border. Conditions in the trenches were appalling. The mud, death and occasional boredom were complemented by lice, rats, and other vermin, worsening the already challenging experience.

The prolonged nature of the conflict meant the British government wanted spiritual succour for its ever-expanding army. In these circumstances, Willie Doyle offered his services as a chaplain. In the early days, volunteering was at a high in both Ireland and Britain, and the presence of chaplains was recognised as a beneficial aid to the morale of the soldiers. Chaplains would provide spiritual accompaniment with liturgies and sacraments where necessary. Some, like Willie Doyle, would go a step further and live with the men in the trenches. This was not a general requirement of chaplains, but it was certainly common among the Jesuit chaplains. Such acts of sacrifice did a lot to endear these chaplains to the men they served alongside.

In 1914 Willie volunteered to be a chaplain. Writing about his decision he says, 'I have volunteered for the Front as a Military Chaplain, though perhaps I may never be sent. Naturally I have little attraction for the hardship and suffering the life would mean; but it is a glorious chance of making the 'ould body' bear something for Christ's dear sake. However, what decided me in the end was the thought that flashed into my mind when in the chapel: the thought that if I get killed I shall die a martyr of charity and so the longing of my heart will be gratified. This much my offering myself as chaplain has done for me: it has made me realise that my life may be very short and that I must do all I can for Jesus now.'[28]

In 1915 Willie's application was accepted, and he found himself in France. He quickly came to see the horrors of war, and shortly after arriving at the front, he came face to face with a gas attack. This was one of the most brutal methods of destruction used during the conflict. Chemical weapons were deployed to kill the opposing side. The effects of gas attacks were often harrowing to witness, and those who survived were left with long-lasting health problems.

28 Patrick Kenny (ed), *To Raise the Fallen: The War Letters, Prayers, and Spiritual Writings of Fr Willie Doyle* (Dublin: Veritas, 2017) , 33.

Willie writes about this experience, saying, 'I had come through the three attacks without ill results, though having been unexpectedly caught in the last one, as I was anointing a dying man and did not see the poisonous fumes coming, I had swallowed some of the gas before I could get my helmet on. It was nothing very serious, but left me rather weak and washy. There was little time to think of that, for wounded and dying were lying all along the trenches. And I was the only priest on that section at that time.'[29]

Even amid the carnage, Willie was with the troops. He never thought of his safety but ensured that spiritual assistance was administered. Even though he put on a cheerful exterior to the soldiers, he was not oblivious to the feelings of fear, as he confides in a letter home,

> The shells were coming over thick and fast now and at last what I expected and feared happened. A big 'crump' hit the wall fair and square, blew three men into the field fifty yards away and buried five others who were in a small dug-out. For a moment I hesitated, for the horrible sight fairly knocked the 'starch' out of me and a couple more 'crumps' did not help to restore my courage. I climbed over the trench and ran across the open, as abject a coward as ever walked on two legs, till I reached the three dying men and then the 'Perfect Trust' came back to me and I felt no fear. A few seconds sufficed to absolve and anoint my poor boys and I jumped to

29 Kenny, *To Raise the Fallen*, 47.

43

my feet, only to go down on my face faster than I
got up, as an 'express train' from Berlin roared by.[30]

His humour shone through in his correspondences. Yes,
he admitted to feeling fear, but even in those moments, he
was still able to hand himself over to God and be present
to those in need. Conditions on the front never improved
for Willie or the troops. Periods of monotony were
broken by commands to charge the German lines. Such
plans were designed to win the war and saw soldiers rush
toward well-defended German lines, getting mowed down
by machinegun fire. Such slaughter did little to alter the
battle lines. Great campaigns launched by the British rarely
achieved their strategic objects, and they could only count
their rare success in terms of feet acquired rather than miles
gained. Still, the madness thundered on.

Writing about his final Christmas Mass, Willie paints
a beautiful scene amongst the destruction taking place
around him, 'I sang the Mass ... One of the Tommies from
Dolphin's Barn, sang the Adeste beautifully, with just a
touch of the sweet Dublin accent to remind us of "home
sweet home", the whole congregation joining the chorus.
It was a curious contrast: the chapel packed with men and
officers, all most strangely quiet and reverent (the nuns
were particularly struck by this) praying and singing most
devoutly, while the big tears ran down many a rough cheek;
outside the cannon boomed and the machine-guns spat out
a hail of lead – peace and good will – hatred and bloodshed!

30   Kenny, *To Raise the Fallen*, 73.

It was a Midnight Mass none of us will ever forget and will certainly live in our memories for many a year. A good 500 men came to Holy Communion, so that I was more than rewarded for my work.'[31]

Even though some respite broke the horror of war, conditions were bleak. Often the living coexisted with the dead, 'I thought our dug-out in one of the trenches at Loos was bad enough. One end of it had been blown in by a big shell, burying two men, whom it was impossible to get out, and we lived at the other. They, poor chaps, were covered with clay, but not deep enough to keep out the smell of decaying bodies, which did not help one's appetite at meal time, and then when your nerves were more jumpy than usual, you could swear you saw the dead man's boot moving, as if he were still alive.'[32]

In the brutal conditions, Willie continued to carry out his priestly ministry, in the hopes of bringing Jesus to the people whom he ministered to, 'It was the feast of Corpus Christi and I thought of the many processions of the Blessed Sacrament being held at that moment all over the world. Surely there never was a stranger one than mine that day as I carried the "God of Consolation" in my unworthy

31   Kenny, *To Raise the Fallen*, 64.
32   Kenny, *To Raise the Fallen*, 68.

arms over the blood-stained battlefield. There was no music to welcome His coming, save the scream of a passing shell; the flowers that strewed His path were the broken bleeding bodies of those for whom he had once died and the only "Altar of Repose" He could find was the heart of one who was working for Him alone, striving in a feeble way to make him some return for all his love and goodness.'[33]

One of the unique things about Willie's chaplaincy was the regard in which Protestant soldiers held him. In the days before ecumenism he practiced it in a way which bore fruit amongst men who would otherwise have been taught to revile a Catholic priest. One Protestant recounted to a fellow Jesuit, 'Another Officer, also a Protestant, said "Fr D. never rests. Night and Day he is with us. He finds a dying or dead man, does all, comes back smiling, makes a little cross and goes out to bury him, and then begins all over again." I needn't say, that through all this, the conditions of the ground and air and discomfort surpass anything that I ever dreamt of in the worst days of the Somme.'[34]

The end came on 16 August 1917 at the Battle of Langemarck. During the battle, two Protestant soldiers had become injured. Willie left the trenches to rescue the men. Upon doing so, he was hit by a German shell and killed. The body was initially recovered. He was recognised by his Pioneer pin.[35] The pin was taken off, and the soldiers planned to return for his body. Upon returning, they

33 Kenny, *To Raise the Fallen*, 74.
34 Hope, *Worshipper and Worshipped*, 657.
35 Symbol of The Pioneer Total Abstinence Association of the Sacred Heart, featuring an image of the Sacred Heart.

discovered that a subsequent German shell had obliterated the body. A testament appeared shortly after his death in a Glasgow newspaper from an anonymous member of the Orange Order.[36]

> God never made a nobler soul. Father Doyle was a good deal amongst us. We could not possibly agree with his religious opinions, but we simply worshipped him for other things. He didn't know the meaning of fear, and he did not know what bigotry was. He was as ready to risk his life and take a drop of water to a wounded Ulsterman as to assist men of his own faith and regiment. If he risked his life in looking after Ulster Protestant soldiers once, he did it a hundred times in the last few days. They told him he was wanted in a more exposed part of the field to administer the last rites of the Church to a fusilier who had been badly hit. In spite of the danger to himself, Father Doyle went over. While he was doing what he could to comfort the poor chap at the very gates of death, the priest was struck down. He and the man he was ministering to passed out of life together. The Ulstermen felt his loss more keenly than anybody, and none more readier to show their marks of respect to the dead hero priest than were our Ulster Presbyterians. Father Doyle was a fine Christian in every sense of the word, and a credit to any religious faith. He

36 Protestant group founded in eighteenth-century Ireland to oppose Catholic Emancipation.

never tried to get things easy. He was always sharing the risks of the men, and had to be kept in restraint by the staff for his own protection. Many a time have I seen him walk beside a stretcher trying to console a wounded man, with bullets flying around him, and shells bursting every few yards.[37]

A fellow Jesuit chaplain, Frank Browne, wrote about Willie after his death, 'All during these last few months he was my greatest help, and to his saintly advice, and still more to his saintly example, I owe everything I felt and did. With him, as with others of us, his bravery was no mere physical show-off. He was afraid and felt fear deeply, how deeply few can realise. And yet the last word said of him to me by the Adjutant of the Royal Irish Rifles in answer to my question, "I hope you are taking care of Fr Doyle?" was, "He is as fond of the shells as ever." His one idea was to do God's work with the men, to make them saints. How he worked and how he prayed for this! Fine weather and foul he was always thinking of them and what he could do for them. In the cold weather he would not use the stove I bought for our dug-out. He scoffed at the idea as making it 'stuffy' – and that when the thermometer was fifteen to twenty degrees below zero, the coldest ever known in living memory here. And how he loathed it all, the life and all it implied! And yet nobody suspected it. God's Will was his law. And to all who remonstrated, "Must I not be about the Lord's business?" was his laughing answer in act and deed

37   Kenny, *To Raise the Fallen*, 188–189.

and not merely in word. May he rest in peace – it seems superfluous to pray for him.'[38]

A Saint?

In the 1930s, the Irish Province sought feedback from Jesuits regarding potential saints. Four names were offered to the Province, including Willie Doyle and John Sullivan. After seeking recommendations, the Province supported the cause of John Sullivan. Despite this, devotion to Willie Doyle has continued to grow. At the time of writing, a lay association has formed in Ireland to promote his cause for canonisation.

38 Kenny, *To Raise the Fallen*, 189–190.

TIME TO REFLECT

Willie showed bravery and a commitment to 'the Lord's business' during the First World War, but he also knew fear. It's time to pause and reflect on the end of Willie's life.

1. Even though he was afraid, Willie remained committed to the spiritual needs of the soldiers in his care. Have you ever had to overcome fear in doing what you felt was right?

2. Willie cared just as much for Protestants as for Catholics. He didn't discriminate. What can you learn from Willie about God's love, which knows no such boundaries?

3. Willie's work and spirituality has inspired so many. Have you been touched by his story? If so, can you integrate his message of love, bravery and tenderness into your own life?

WHAT CAN WILLIE DOYLE TEACH PEOPLE TODAY?

OVER ONE hundred years on from his death in the First World War, Willie Doyle, continues to fascinate people. Some have focused on his tenderness, others his sense of humour; for some his bravery is inspiring, and others are interested in his spirituality. Looking back at Willie's life, what lessons does he have for the world of today?

Lesson One: Helping Others

Willie lived his life for other people. Even from his earliest days, he was always putting others needs before his own. He was born into a privileged family in Dublin and had access to many of the finer things that life had to offer. Despite this he had a great interest in assisting those who were less well off. As a boy, he would get up early in the morning and complete work that was typically done by domestic staff. When young Willie was given money for sweets, he would seek out people that were in need and give the money to them.

This sense of charity continued into adulthood, where he played an essential part in the life of the soldiers he served alongside in the First World War. Willie, as a chaplain, could have avoided the front lines, but he chose instead to be with the soldiers. On one occasion, he even allowed a doctor to sleep on his back to save the man from having to rest on the wet floor of a trench. Willie's desire to be with the soldiers in these appalling conditions resulted in his eventual death. He regularly ventured onto the battlefield to try and rescue injured soldiers; it was on such a mission that he lost his life.

In today's world this kind of selflessness is becoming rarer than ever. Willie's life is a reminder that there is more to life than selfishness – all of the People of God are called to be 'about the Lord's business'.

Lesson Two: A Sense of Fun

Willie loved practical jokes, and this resulted in mixed opinions of him. He was quite popular with students during his time as a teacher. They appreciated his capacity for practical jokes. His Jesuit colleagues, who were often the butt of his jokes, were less enthusiastic. One of his recorded gags involved dressing up an object as a priest and allowing it to fall out a window, making those watching think he himself had fallen.

Despite his humour Willie lived a rigorous life of penance. This was something he took on board personally and was not something he ever forced on others. There was no conflict between Willie's personal commitment to this penance and his good humour.

Christians have good reason to celebrate! Pope Francis has said that many Christians have a 'face of sadness', a face from a 'funeral wake'.[39] For some, there is no sense of the joy of the resurrection in their spirituality. Willie's sense of fun was something that drew people to him all throughout his life. He has shown that good humour and joyousness even in difficult circumstances is important to the Christian life.

Lesson Three: Jesuit Spirituality Is for Everyone

The Spiritual Exercises of Ignatius are a popular way of praying today. At the turn of the twentieth century, they were almost the exclusive preserve of priests and religious. The Exercises made such a profound impact on Willie that he felt they should be available to the largest audience possible. He helped to make retreats based on the Exercises widely accessible to lay people, in particular working-class people.

> There was no conflict between Willie's personal commitment to this penance and his good humour.

This approach to spirituality was influential in developing a future retreat ministry that saw the expansion of the Spiritual Exercises to the broadest possible audience. It helped open the doors for everyone to appreciate the value

39 Pope Francis, *Angelus: 13/20/2022* (Vatican: The Holy See, 2020), www.vatican.va/content/francesco/en/angelus/2020/documents/papa-francesco_angelus_20201213.html.

of Ignatius's wisdom and know that they too could grow closer to God by following his example. Such was Willie's admiration for the Spiritual Exercises. He knew that they could be transformative in the lives of others.

Willie's life has shown that Jesuit spirituality is for everyone.

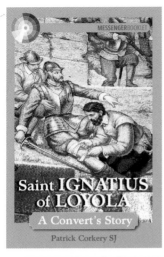

MESSENGER**BOOKLET**

Saint **IGNATIUS** of **LOYOLA**
A Convert's Story

Patrick Corkery SJ

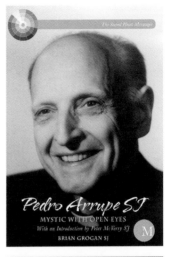

The Sacred Heart Messenger

Pedro Arrupe SJ
MYSTIC WITH OPEN EYES
With an Introduction by Peter McVerry SJ
BRIAN GROGAN SJ

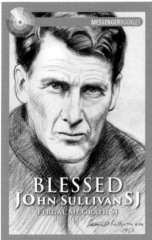

MESSENGER**BOOKLET**

BLESSED **JOHN SULLIVAN SJ**
FERGAL McGRATH SJ

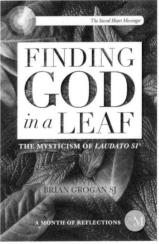

The Sacred Heart Messenger

FINDING **GOD** *in a* **LEAF**
THE MYSTICISM OF *LAUDATO SI'*

BRIAN GROGAN SJ

A MONTH OF REFLECTIONS

www.messenger.ie